KU-655-619

DROUGHT

Heinemann
LIBRARY

Catherine Chambers

www.heinemann.co.uk/library

Visit our website to find out more information about **Heinemann Library** books.

To order:

 Phone ++44 (0)1865 888066

 Send a fax to ++44 (0)1865 314091

 Visit the Heinemann Bookshop at www.heinemann.co.uk/library to browse our catalogue and order online.

First published in Great Britain by Heinemann Library, Halley Court, Jordan Hill, Oxford OX2 8EJ, a division of Reed Educational and Professional Publishing Ltd. Heinemann is a registered trademark of Reed Educational & Professional Publishing Ltd.

OXFORD MELBOURNE AUCKLAND JOHANNESBURG BLANTYRE
GABORONE IBADAN PORTSMOUTH NH (USA) CHICAGO

Designed by Visual Image
Illustration by Paul Bale
Originated by Ambassador Litho Ltd.
Printed and bound in South China.

ISBN 0 431 15067 2

06 05 04 03 02
10 9 8 7 6 5 4 3 2 1

British Library Cataloguing in Publication Data

Chambers, Catherine
Drought. – (Wild Weather)
1. Droughts – Juvenile literature
I. Title
551.5'773
ISBN 0431150672

Acknowledgements

The Publishers would like to thank the following for permission to reproduce photographs: Ardea p4, Associated Press p17, Bruce Coleman Collection p10, Corbis pp13, 22, 24, 25, 26, 29, Ecoscene p28, Eye Ubiquitous p20, FLPA p19, Photodisc pp8, 21, Robert Harding Picture Library pp7, 12, 14, 23, Science Photo Library p18, Still Pictures pp5, 11, Stone (Getty) p15, Stock Market p9, TRH p27.

The Publishers would like to thank the Met Office for their assistance with the preparation of this book.

Cover photograph reproduced with permission of Topham Picturepoint.

Every effort has been made to contact copyright holders of any material reproduced in this book. Any omissions will be rectified in subsequent printings if notice is given to the Publisher.

Any words appearing in the text in bold, **like this**, are explained in the Glossary.

Contents

What is drought?

A drought happens when people expect rain but it does not come. There is no water anywhere. Land, rivers and lakes dry out.

Crops need water to grow. If there is no
water they cannot grow. People and animals
have no food to eat or water to drink.
Sometimes they die.

Where does drought happen?

In **deserts** there is hardly any rain. Drought happens a lot on the edges of deserts. Sometimes rain doesn't fall at all. The land becomes very dry.

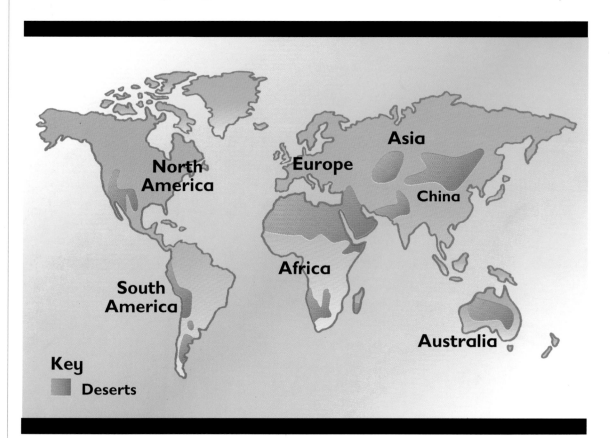

North America

Europe

Asia

China

Africa

South America

Australia

Key
Deserts

Drought can also happen far away from deserts. It can happen in wetter parts of Australia, during a very hot, dry summer.

Why doesn't the rain fall?

Rain falls from **clouds**. Clouds hold **water vapour**, which is a gas. The sky high up gets very cold. It cools the water vapour and turns it into drops of water. These drops fall as rain.

When the sky is clear there are no clouds, so there is no rain. The air is very dry. There are also no clouds to stop the heat of the Sun from drying out the earth.

9

Why do droughts happen?

Drought happens when rain **clouds** do not form for a long time. Sometimes people can plan for the dry weather. At other times dry weather can bring drought **disaster**.

Drought is made worse when people cut down
too many trees. Trees put **moisture** into the air
and give shade from the Sun. Their roots hold
the soil together.

What are droughts like?

During a drought the earth becomes dry and cracked. Soil turns to dust and blows around in the dry wind. Leaves turn yellow. Flowers and fruit droop and **wither**.

The water in rivers, lakes and **reservoirs** gets lower and lower. Only mud is left. Fish, frogs and plants cannot **survive**. Animals have to travel a long way to find water to drink.

Harmful drought

People need water for drinking, cooking and washing. Drought dries up the water supplies. In some places the drinking water becomes dirty. This can bring **disease**.

Grasses, trees and bushes dry out in a drought.
Dry **vegetation** catches fire very easily. This
can lead to huge forest fires. Forest fires can kill
people, animals and plants.

Drought in the Sahel

This map shows a place where drought often happens – the African Sahel. The Sahel is a very dry part of Africa. There is usually just enough rain for **crops** to grow.

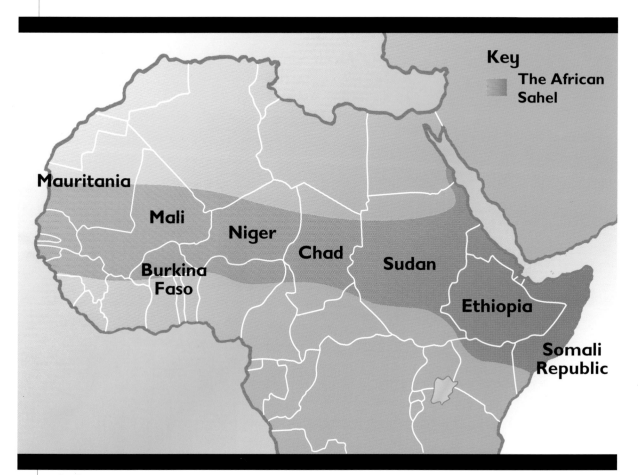

Key
The African Sahel

Mauritania

Mali

Niger

Burkina Faso

Chad

Sudan

Ethiopia

Somali Republic

Here in the Sahel a drought has killed the grass. These animals have nothing to eat. This means that they might die. People in the Sahel need the animals for meat and milk.

Preparing for drought

Pictures taken by **satellites**, from space, track clear skies over the Earth. They also show where lakes and rivers are drying out. Scientists use the pictures to help them **predict** drought.

People in dry areas try to save water in case there is a drought. They collect rainwater in tanks. Waste water in towns and cities is cleaned and used again.

Coping with drought

People collect rainwater in **reservoirs**. Then they have enough water even if there has not been any rain. During a bad drought, reservoirs can become empty.

Water hoses and sprinklers use a lot of water. Gardeners are told not to use them in a drought.

Coping with drought in the Sahel

A terrible drought came to the African Sahel in the 1980s. People ate all the cereal **crops** saved in their **grain** stores. Then they sold their farm animals to buy food.

All the food ran out. So governments and **aid agencies** set up food camps. People walked a long way to reach them. Many people still died from hunger and **disease**.

How do animals and plants cope?

In Australia, cows and sheep graze far away from the farm. In a drought they cannot find grass or water. So farm workers bring them food and water on trucks.

Millet is a cereal grown for food. It grows
well in dry places. Millet has a tough waxy
stem and long thin leaves. These do not lose
much **moisture**.

To the rescue!

Aid workers bring people food in a drought. They also bring equipment to make water safe to drink. Dirty water can carry **diseases**.

Firefighters help people to escape from forest fires before the flames burn their homes. Fire engines and aircraft then put out the fire. The aircraft bomb the fire with water.

Adapting to drought

In Egypt farmers can grow **crops** in a drought. They collect the waters of the huge River Nile in a man-made lake. This is called a dam. The water in the dam helps their crops to grow.

Ethiopia is a country in the African Sahel.
It suffers badly from drought. So people are
growing thousands of trees. These help to hold
the soil together and stop the earth from
drying out.

Fact file

◆ China and India have had the worst droughts ever. They happened over 100 years ago in the 1870s and 1880s. Many millions of people died.

◆ Drought can bring huge dust storms. Masses of tiny dust **particles** can travel thousands of miles. They are carried by winds high up in the sky.

◆ There was a drought in the United Kingdom in the summer of 1976. Thousands of ladybirds hatched out in the heat. They swarmed over people lying on the beach. The summer became known as 'Ladybird Summer'.

Glossary

aid agencies groups of people who help those suffering from drought

cloud mass of water vapour up in the sky

crops plants grown for eating, like rice or wheat

desert areas of the world that are always very dry

disaster something very bad

disease illness

grain seed heads of grasses

moisture dampness

particles very tiny parts

predict to tell when something is going to happen

reservoirs lakes made by people to store water

satellite spacecraft that moves around the Earth

survive stay alive

vegetation plants such as trees, bushes and grass

water vapour water that has changed into a light gas

wither dry out and shrink

Index